Vantage Point

A New View of Rest, Rhythm, and the Work of God

Brenda Jank

This book was made possible by
the amazing pursuit of our Mighty God and
a team of dedicated, passionate Kingdom workers:
Bethany Andrews, Paige Craig, Dani Kiefer, Rachel Lance
(1st printing)
Dawn Limmer, Melissa McKenzie, Laura Pounds (2nd printing)
through an army of prayer warriors and financial supporters,
with the on-going encouragement of Brenda's husband, Tim,
and their five kids
Joshua, Samuel, Joseph, Anna, and Noah
who find mom a whole lot more fun to live with when she's
running the race she's been called to run and enjoying the
rest she's meant to enjoy.

We value your insights and your stories. We invite you to join the conversation. Visit the website and subscribe to the blog. Short, encouraging devotions will be sent to you each week as you pursue God's gift of rest and rhythm. Onward!

RunHardRestWell.com

Rest

Rest is not a reward.
You can't earn it.
You don't deserve it.
It's a given. A gift. Free of charge and full of grace. It pours into our lives from the heart of God.
Rest is a part of His plan. It speaks of quality-control about the race we've been asked to run.
Rest comes to us signed, sealed, delivered, but it is rejected and neglected again and again.
Are you numbered in those ranks?
We all are—if we're honest.
We are made for more, yet settle for less.
Made for more.
The *more* we find in rest invites us to enter a mystery few explore.
It invades our overload.
It makes life right, full and free.
It sets a course for purpose, passion, power.
It's not a sign of weakness or inability, despite what we've come to believe.
Choosing to realign our lives to a rhythm of work *and* rest is a sacred act of defiance, devotion and deliverance.
Rest stands on the threshold.
Hope opens the door.

Welcome

This book can change your life.

Its mission is clear.

***Run Hard. Rest Well.* champions rest to empower God's people to live healthy, vibrant, Kingdom-focused lives**.

This is a book to be read and wrestled with by individuals, then shared with your staff, team or small group. It's a six-week commitment.

The transformative value of this study will be vastly unique for each person involved. It is not a cookie-cutter approach. Its measure cannot come by comparison to others. The insights you glean will challenge your perceptions about rest *and* work. The biblical insights will alter the terrain of your soul. They will alter the impact you have on the Kingdom of God. They will shape those in your sphere of influence. They will transform how your family lives and loves. The rewards will require great intent and determination, but they are sweet and more bountiful than you can ever imagine.

Run hard. Rest well.

Brenda

Table of Contents

For Small Group Leaders

Dear Friend,

You are about to become a hero.

People are drowning. Overload and exhaustion are constant and real. It's dismantling our dreams, our families, and our hope for a better tomorrow. We are tired.

God has a message of help, hope and healing for tired people. It's inviting, transformational and accessible – but it needs a conduit. This small group will be that conduit. And there's good news! You do not have to be an expert on the topic of rest and rhythm, you must simply be courageous – courageous enough to take off your mask. What your group needs most is a safe place to be honest and transparent. Overload does a number on our lives. We need a place where we can be real. Transformation requires transparency. Transparency requires safe people.

As you begin, frame this journey with grace. It's taken us years (decades) to get into the mess of chronic overload and exhaustion, it's going to take more than 6-7 small group sessions to get us out. A new, strong foundation must be laid, and this small group experience will do just that – and more.

Vantage Point is both a personal study guide and small group Bible study. When people commit to both aspects, sparks fly and a refining fire gives birth to something new and beautiful.

Whether you meet once a week, twice a month or once a month, this Small Group Guide can be packaged for your group in 6 or 7 sessions/gatherings. As you invite people to join the group, let them know that there is "homework – 4 personal devotions" to do before each small group gathering.

This guide is built for busy people who want to turn the tide.
• It includes personal work – 4 devotions to digest before every small group gathering.

• It includes group work – which is shared together through the 6 chapters of the book.

Gathering	7-Week Plan	6-Week Plan
Prep	No prep needed	Pass out Guides before you meet. Ask the group to read the INTRO & the 4 Devos of the first chapter.
#1	Read INTRO together. Pass out the Guides.	Chapter 1 Connection
#2	Chapter 1 Connection	Chapter 2 Connection
#3	Chapter 2 Connection	Chapter 3 Connection
#4	Chapter 3 Connection	Chapter 4 Connection
#5	Chapter 4 Connection	Chapter 5 Connection
#6	Chapter 5 Connection	Chapter 6 Connection
#7	Chapter 6 Connection	

The Vantage Point study guide travels the globe. You and your group will be joining believers from all over the world who are committed to reclaiming what God says about the power and purpose of work, rest and rhythm.

Run hard. Break a sweat.
Rest well. Rest as if your life and your work depend on it – for it does!

Onward.
Eyes on Jesus!

Brenda

The Expedition

In everyone's life there are situations and discoveries that transform us. They distance us from what is familiar and open the door to something new and better. The truth behind *Run hard. Rest well* (RHRW) may be one such discovery. It has been for me.

The purpose of this short book is to invite readers to explore the power and purpose of rest, trading our exhaustion and overload for a rhythm that infuses our work and our rest with vision, energy and joy. Rest is not the reward of work well done. Rest positions us for purpose. It's the launching pad, a portal into who we are and what we have been called to do through the power and by the grace of God. Although our definition of "work" may need some fine tuning, our understanding of "rest" typically requires a complete overhaul. Faulty assumptions must be demolished and a solid, Truth-infused foundation must be laid.

Rome was not built in a day. This overhaul will require a journey. For some, it will be a solitary trek, but I encourage you to consider this an expedition. An expedition is a journey undertaken with a group of people. It's a journey framed by community. Through community (with your staff, a team, another person, or your small group) our authenticity is more poignant. Our joy is multiplied. Our challenges are met head-on with prayer, support and encouragement. Our goal is to discover healthy, holy ways to navigate the attractions and distractions of our 24/7 world in light of biblical Truth, the glory of God and our desire for purpose, vibrancy and freedom.

This book was written with specific goals, promises, hopes and expectations in mind.

My Goal:

Create awareness
Share insights and practical suggestions
Spotlight God's promises
Cast a vision
Get out of the way

My Promise:

I will honor ...

... your time. Each devotional chapter is short and sweet. I have a great respect for the moments you spend with this material. Your time is precious. It will not be wasted.

... your intellect. There is no one-size-fits-all mentality about rest. I will not attempt to spoon-feed you. There will be no 10-quick-step formulas. This book offers food for thought, biblical insight, meaningful stories and questions that require reflection.

... your season of life. Learning how to rest is an ongoing process. The journey toward rhythm meets our most pressing needs from a variety of angles – angles that shift and change through planned and unplanned transitions of life. It is my hope that the truths in this book speak boldly and compassionately to people from ages 15 to 95.

My Hope:

My hope is that the message *Run hard. Rest well* will provide a means of escape from the vise-grip of overload. I want it to provide an arena of growth where a wrestling match ensues between cultural norms and biblical truths. A crisis needs to take place. Our fundamental (and typically faulty) beliefs about work and rest must be challenged, spotlighted and demolished, replaced with Truth that comes from the heart of God.

My hope is that this exploration will include others from your life (a friend, a ministry team, staff, small group) with whom you can share this journey. It's a steep climb. The vistas and summits are amazing, but learning how to rest well is one of the most daunting tasks you'll ever face. Accountability is required. Encouragement is mandatory. Countercultural work is best done in groups. We cover a lot of territory when committed to cheering each other on.

My Expectation:

Rest is for all. No one is immune from the staggering price-tag associated with its neglect. In ancient times, rest was reserved only for the rich and famous. God says, "it's for all." Sabbath Keeping is a hallmark feature of Judaism; through the Jewish nation God blessed all the people of the world by speaking to the patterns of rhythm, rest and restoration He established in creation.

People of all ages find aspects of work and rest uniquely attractive or distracting depending on their personality and/or the season of their life. Unique needs are met by rest during different stages of life.

Below is a list of people. For each group I share a unique feature, which speaks to the *obstacles* of rest or the *blessings* found in rest. If time allows, read the whole list. If not, be selective. No matter who you are, you might find that these obstacles and blessings are not confined to any one age, stage or season.

Leaders and Influencers

Our fatigue is an unspoken badge of honor, yet it dismantles our highest priorities. Revolutionizing the way we work and rest will not happen without an intentional championing of rest by leaders committed to bringing out the best in those they lead, for the sake of those they serve. You are in a position to teach your team how to navigate 24/7 from a place of joy, strength, clarity and intimacy with God, but the journey must first be yours.

Men

Focus. We tend to have a singular focus in life. For some, it's work. For some, it's play. Exploring rhythm gives us a new lens through which to view the world.

Women

Guilt. Guilt drives many of the decisions we make and is a faulty, foundational belief behind the profound state of our unrest. When we even begin to slow down, does guilt rise up to nip at our heels and our heart?

Young Adults

Vocational insight. Life-sustaining rhythm. Patterns and mindsets are being established right now. Do we have a vision for biblical wellness? Do I desire something better, different than the exhaustion and overload I see all around me?

Teens

Plugged in. It's the only way of life we've ever known. Life values are being shaped by cell phones. What questions need to be asked? Discussed? Debated? What's at stake? How will we live? What will shape our soul?

Children

Gurus of play! Boxes. Bubbles. Balls. Butterflies. May we, as adults, nurture in you the power of play so that together we may rediscover how to laugh and love again.

Camp Directors

We are uniquely positioned to swing a door wide open for the Body of Christ to recognize the sanctity of sacred space, place and pace through a ministry of retreat – most specifically, personal retreat. Will we cross the threshold ourselves – and hold the door open for those we are positioned to serve and invite?

Caregivers of Special-Needs Children & Aging Loved Ones

We are privileged to love people who need more, take more <u>and</u> give more than most will ever know. These labors of love are staggering *and* treasure-filled. Recognizing rest, respite and retreat as strategic priorities are a life-giving paradigm shift that will position us to thrive through intense seasons of loving full-tilt.

Older Adults

Peering into the rear-view mirror is precious time well-spent, but the Lord is not done with us. We have gifts to share, talents to use, passions to express. We can't be content with the self-indulgence of the American dream. God has more in mind for us.

Those in Crisis

Two common denominators in life are crisis and heartache. These come wrapped in hundreds of ways through a thousand different events and burdens. No matter our heartache, facing disappointment (moderate to crushing) is a part of the process, be it the staggering loss of love, control, dignity, hope, or all of the above. Learning how to *rest well* builds margin into our lives, allowing us the time we need to grieve, heal and grow.

Do you see yourself in this list? I do. Every single one.

So, Who Am I?

My name is Brenda. I am a child of God, the founder and forger of *Run Hard. Rest Well* and mom in a family of seven. My journey into the rhythms of rest began when I was single, took off during the first years of marriage, was derailed when our first three were in diapers, and then over time, became firmly established as we moved from life with toddlers into a life with teens. I live an ordinary life with an extraordinary God.

My husband, Tim, directs a Christian camp and retreat center in northeast Indiana. We have five children, a crazy crew of some of God's finest and feistiest. Four of our kids have significant medical needs and challenges. We know the joys of adoption. Our life is routinely unpredictable. It's a wild ride in the best of times. Through it, despite it, and because of it, we are refined by fire and held tight in the grip of grace. Our children are the reason I am committed to intentional rhythms of rest. I would not be here without these rhythms – and neither would they. We'd all be buried six feet under.

I champion rest. I equip people to rediscover the power and purpose of rhythm and rest so that we might be more passionate and more prepared to be about God's work on earth. I live in the trenches, desiring God's ongoing work to be fully released in my life. My commitment to rest is fueled by a home-grown desire to live and love with joy and delight. Join the journey. It's an adventure and an invitation to the life God wants us to live.

Make it Your Own

With which groups do you most readily identify in this season of your life?

1 Rest 101
Vantage Point | Trek 1

Culture and Rhythm

Our culture does not promote, encourage or provide for sustainability. Three dynamics come into play in the Western mindset: We work hard. We play hard. And we overdose on almost everything we get our hands on.

We work hard

The Puritan work ethic has shaped American culture. We are people who applaud productivity. There is nothing wrong with this – at all! It's an outstanding quality, one that seeks to combine creativity, vision and stamina to build great things. We just can't do it at a pace that dismantles the priorities we hold dear. There must be established limits that are honored and valued. Our work – and our rest – depend on it.

We play hard

Devoid of a solid, biblical understanding of rest, we have come to define "rest" as "play." Enjoying favorite pastimes (basketball, cooking, running, movies, etc.) is a part of rest, no doubt, but it's not the bottom line. Entertainment and social media dominate the landscape of our time and our lives. It's a black hole, which sucks unsuspecting people into its vortex. Knowing how and when to play is vital to our health and well-being, but so is learning how and when to rest.

> **Our culture does not promote, encourage or provide for sustainability.**

Rest. What is it?

Rest is a major theme gracing the pages of God's Word, no matter how little it is currently gracing our lives; but what does it look like?

Rest is best understood in terms of rhythm. The Bible highlights four rhythms of rest and restoration. These four rhythms create a framework for us to build vibrancy and sustainability into the core of our being. They are simple, obvious and divinely orchestrated, yet rarely seen as a collective whole. Having no mentors in the arena of rest, these four rhythms have given me a *model* and the *method* of rest. They answer important questions we rarely ask. What is rest? What does it look like? What does it create and accomplish in my life?

These four rhythms, seen as a package deal, identify four critical needs that define us as human beings. God is infinite. We are not. We have limits. He does not. Recognizing our needs and limits is a crucial first step. There are limits to our physical ability to tackle the demands and opportunities before us. There are also emotional, spiritual and relational limits to those same tasks and dreams.

Our tanks run dry. This is not sin, this is humanity – as God planned it. Our needs, when recognized and honored, create a deep dependence on God. This dependence will define who we are and our impact on the Kingdom. When we embrace this

> Our needs, when recognized and honored, create a deep dependence on God.

dependence, we soar to great heights. If we demand independence, resisting limits and refusing restorative rhythms, we crash and burn. For some it will be a public spectacle, but for most, it will be a painful, lonely, personal demise.

The rhythms we see in God's Word meet our four basic needs for rest: physical, emotional, spiritual and relational.
The first two rhythms are visible throughout the entire Bible. They make their debut, however, in the Old Testament's account of Creation: Sabbath and sleep.

The other two rhythms, also visible throughout Scripture, are clearly seen in the four Gospel accounts of the New Testament. They were modeled by Jesus when He walked this earth: stillness (personal prayer) and solitude (personal retreat).

Four rhythms of restoration rise to the surface as we explore power and purpose of rest.

Find rest, O my soul, in God alone; my hope comes from Him. Ps 62:5

Daily Rhythms
Sleep
Sleep is a daily rhythm established in creation. Designed to **refresh** us (in ways we are only beginning to fully understand), it meets our *physical* need for rest. Our expedition into the rhythms of rest will help us recognize and honor the fact that our need for sleep is not a design flaw.

Refresh.
Renew.
Replenish.
Rejuvenate.

Stillness (personal prayer)

Stillness is a daily rhythm highlighted through the life of Christ. Designed to renew us, it meets our spiritual need for rest, a rest spotlighted in Psalm 62:5 NIV. "Find rest, O my soul, in God alone; my hope comes from Him." Our expedition into the rhythms of rest will help us recognize and honor the power of planned and unplanned time for personal prayer. "Be still and know that I am God..." Psalm 46:10 NIV. To "be still" is a purposeful pause in the Presence of God.

Weekly Rhythm
Sabbath

Sabbath is a weekly rhythm established in creation. Designed to replenish, it meets our relational needs to reconnect with God and those we love. Our expedition into the rhythms of restoration will help us recognize and honor Sabbath as a deliberate, intentional pause from our work to "pray and play." Released from everyday demands and burdens, we are positioned to fully and freely celebrate our relationship with the Living God and celebrate the love we share with those He's placed in our lives. It's a day of delight and devotion.

Seasonal Rhythm
Solitude (personal retreat)

Solitude is an intentional rhythm highlighted in the life of Christ. Designed to rejuvenate and empower us in quiet places off the beaten path (lasting hours or days), it meets our need for emotional rest. Our expedition

into the rhythms of restoration
 will help us recognize and honor the fact
that personal retreat is the pursuit of God
off the beaten path, away from the demands
and distractions of everyday life.

Make it Your Own

• What does our culture tell us about work, play, and rest? Do these values honor God?

• Which rhythm of rest do you engage in with the greatest ease? With the most resistance?

The Rhythms of Rest

Sleep

Sabbath Keeping

Stillness (personal prayer)

Solitude (personal retreat)

Price Tag

There is a price to be paid for our chronic exhaustion. For some people, it's apparent in the here and now: fleeting joy, fragmented relationships, growing irritability. Sometimes it comes and goes: bouts of sleepless nights, depression, illness. Some people seemingly sail through their overload, but the price tag is high when they die prematurely, five, 15 or 30 years earlier than they should.

What do I need? What do I want? Am I willing to pay the price?

What's the cost of your overload? Is it worth the price tag?

Three important questions come to mind when I take a look at the state of my exhaustion.

What do I need?
What do I want?
Am I willing to pay the price?

What do I need? A lot. The dentist tells me I need to floss. My doctor tells me I need to lose 15 pounds. The government tells me I need to pay my taxes. My kids tell me I need to dye the gray out of my hair, oh, and drive them to 16 practices and activities this week.

Since our basic needs for clean water, food, safety and shelter are typically met, most of my needs are really a matter of wants. My wants are driven by 1) my pursuit of a reward or 2) my desire to avoid negative consequences.

Seeking the reward – or suffering the 0
The real question behind needs and wants
in modern society is: Am I willing to pay the
price?

There is a price to be paid for our
exhaustion.
There is a price to be paid for our
restoration.

Rest does not come free. It requires a
radical revision of thinking and beliefs.
It demands an alteration of how life
unfolds. The cost is high. It's painful
to face the reality of our own limits. It's
brutal to disappoint others and perhaps,
even harder to disappoint ourselves. But
the consequences of not tending to our
basic needs for rest are staggering. The
rewards, however, are truly beyond our
comprehension. They are out of this world –
in more ways than one. The first step on the
journey toward rest and restoration is a very
short inventory and assessment. James A.
Garfield once said, "The truth will set you
free, but first it might make you miserable."
This inventory is short. Very short. I hate
tests. I hate the time they take. I also
recognize test anxiety. When I take a test,
I know what an inventory is looking for, so
authentic results can be easily skewed. I've
kept this in mind, in case you're like me.

> **"When I choose to rest, I am participating in what God calls holy."**

Assessment

Are you happy?

> (Joy, yes. But do you laugh? Have fun? Can you be playful?)

Are you healthy?

> (Are you habits conducive to good health? Sleep, food, exercise?)

Are you holy?

> (Are you growing? What about self-control, patience, goodness, love...)

Are you whole?

> (Are there any gaps between your public and private world? Are you key relationships healthy, strong, maturing?)

The real key to this four-question assessment is to hand it off to someone who knows you well. It may give you a more accurate (however painful) assessment. It also might launch a very intriguing conversation. Do you dare? Give it a try.

Inventory

Place a check mark in front of every statement that is 100% true. This is a snapshot of your life today, not for all time and eternity. It gives you information about this specific season of your life. It does not label or define you. It is a snapshot. Be honest.

1 _____ In the last four weeks, I've enjoyed four days off – days that were refreshing and care-free.

2 _____ This past week I've had five nights of sleep that were 7 to 8 hours in duration.

3 _____ I experience the Presence of God on a regular basis in personal devotions.

4 _____ I took a full day of personal retreat in the last six months.

_____ I enjoyed four evenings this past week with no out-of-the-home
5 _____ obligations.
6 _____ I took all my vacation time last year.
_____ **Total check-marks**

Scores

Score: 0-3 – You are running on the fumes of an empty tank whether you realize it or not. There's a better way. It's found in the rhythm *Run hard. Rest well.* A paradigm shift must take place in your heart. Rest is not a sign of weakness. It is a gift, a grace, a rhythm of life for those who surrender all – including the time it takes to rest. The vibrancy of your ministry, the well-being of your soul and the health of your family depend on it.

Score: 4 – You are familiar with the rejuvenating aspects of rest and renewal ("Well done, good and faithful servant!"), but gaps remain. You know how to run hard and you are aware of what it means to rest well. Now take a look at your physical, emotional, spiritual, relational reserves. What are your strengths? Where can you improve? Expand your horizons. What needs attention? Explore how "resting well" will bring new realms of vibrancy to an area where you're serving with a self-imposed limp.

Score: 5-6 – Ah! The life-giving rhythms of rest are established in your life. You have adopted God's ways and not the world's. The fruit of well-being is yours to enjoy – and pass along to others. Stay the course. Your life is a walking billboard. Be intentional about sharing the story of your journey into the rhythms of rest. You have a remarkable opportunity to light the way.

Rest. Do you need it? Do you want it? Are you willing to pay the price it requires?

This week, would you be willing to accept a challenge of setting aside a block of time (two to three hours) to rest? The only requirement of this time is to do something that brings delight. Get outside. Turn off your phone. Release yourself from all demands. Splurge on a special cup of coffee. Meet a friend. Make a date with your pillow. Take a walk. Step into this time guilt-free. Plan for it. Anticipate it. Guard it. Why?

Because rest is holy.

The first thing God called holy was not Himself, not the act of worship or the splendor of creation. The first thing God called holy was time set apart to rest (Genesis 2:3).

When I choose to rest, I am participating in what God calls holy.
Rest. Do you need it? Do you want it? Are you willing to pay the price to embrace it?

Make it Your Own

• How hard or easy was it to be honest with your inventory and assessment?

• Does Genesis 2:3 alter your view of rest?

Roadblocks

Buried in the collective mindset of Western culture and deep within our own hearts is the notion that rest is not an activity for the movers and shakers of this world. Rest is not for the vibrant and passionate, but for the decrepit who live in "rest homes" and for the dead who we encourage to "rest in peace."

Still, we all can attest to a very real need for rest. It bears down upon us with a crushing force. So we flirt with rest. Entertainment and escape top the list. Entertainment is made up of socially acceptable activities like TV, movies, sporting events, shopping, gaming, social media, etc. These activities can be a part of rest, when enjoyed in moderation. Too often, however, they are the sole beneficiaries of our attention. In excessive doses, these activities are not God-honoring and do not refresh, recharge or refuel.

Escape is another thing. These activities – often addictions – are socially unacceptable by most standards. There is a darkness to escape. These activities are often done in secret and we become caught in their grip. In the end they leave us empty and reeling, unraveling all we hold dear.

Why do entertainment and escape get the best of our "free" time? Because we do not have a theology of rest. This lack, this loss, this gap, causes us to fall back on the

Rest is doing that which refreshes.

definition of rest sculpted and crafted by the world, a definition focused on entertainment and escape.

What is your definition of rest? Have you ever spent time thinking that through?

When we dig a little deeper, we must explore the factors that influence our definition of rest.

There are six heavy hitters:

1. **The Puritan Work Ethic** – America was founded on a value of work. It has been chiseled into the core of our being. Hard work and delayed rewards built a strong, growing economy over the last two hundred years. This value of work is seen in our ideas concerning vacation. Many Americans are excited about getting away for a long weekend. Many Europeans on the other hand, value vacations lasting two, three, four weeks in length. Different mindsets. Different values.

2. **Home Life** – Did your parents place a high value on work and accomplishment? Or did they have a more relaxed approach to life? There's a good chance their values rubbed off on you. More is caught than taught. There's a good chance, too, that if your parents valued hard work, your sense of self-esteem might hinge on your sense of accomplishment. Is that true for you?

Your Personality – We are wired from birth; fearfully and wonderfully made. Are you known more (not exclusively) for being "responsible and organized" or "fun-loving, relaxed and imaginative?" Both tendencies have unique gifts to offer the world of work and rest. You were born with

a natural **bent.** Understanding that bent
and the deeply held convictions it breeds is
important work on the journey of learning
how to *Run hard. Rest well.*

4. **The Church** – The church teaches us to love, serve, forgive,
    tithe, and pray, but have you ever been taught how to rest?
    Rest well? It's an area where the church falls painfully short.
    Rest is not valued, prioritized or modeled by our leaders and
    mentors. Few take this road less traveled, so we wander in
    the desert weary and worn.

5. **Our Disregard and Contempt for Limits** – Mindy
    Caliguire, founder of Soul Care, reminds us that our "refusal
    to live within our 'God-designed' limits is the root of many
    evils in our lives." Here's my favorite quote from her:

    > *Do I frequently desire to be more than I am? My calendar
    > reveals this issue in my life. When scheduling I'm not always
    > realistic about the limits of my time or energy. And as a
    > result, my 'masked' self (super-human self), who does not
    > want to disappoint others or wishes to appear more capable,
    > says "yes" to too many things. My 'masked' self has agreed
    > to something my real self cannot sustain. As hard as it is
    > for me to face, this kind of refusal to live within my 'God-
    > designed' limits is the root of many evils in my life (creating
    > for me a life that is) unmanageable at a level far deeper than
    > the appearance of*
    > *my closets.*

    Amen to that! We have to ask ourselves, "Do I consider my
    need for rest and replenishment a design flaw?" It's one of
    the most important questions I've had to ask myself and
    I've had to ask it more than once.

6. **The Myth of a Calmer Tomorrow** – We've all said
    it. We all believe it. "I'll take a break when ... this project
    wraps up ... when the kids are back in school ... when
    Christmas is over ... when summer is over ..." We try to

convince ourselves that the end of "this madness, this relentless pace" is in sight. But that hope forever lingers on the horizon, eternally out of our grasp.

Rest. A definition I've come to live by is very simple. *Rest is doing that which refreshes.* This idea was planted by God in my heart through Moses in Exodus 23:12 NIV. It resonates deep within.

> *Six days do your work, but on the seventh day do not work, so that ... (all) may be refreshed.*

Make it Your Own

• What is your definition of rest? What does rest look like in your life?

• What roadblocks stand in your way? External realities play a role (no doubt), but how often are we hindered by internal beliefs and acquired baggage? What role do these play in your unrest?

Guilt 101

In the last months of her life, I met a woman named Kathryn, wife and mother of two lovely young girls. Kathryn was fighting colon cancer. We were both newcomers to a Sunday morning Bible study. Her family was new to Indiana. My family was new to the church. I found Kathryn's approach to life captivating. I wanted to get to know her, but I was hesitant. Wouldn't she be guarded with her days?

"Kathryn, could we have lunch sometime?"

"Oh, Brenda, I would love to. For the first time in my life, I am a person with time."

My surprise over the use of her words, "I am a person with time" must have registered on my face. She smiled warmly and placed her hand on my arm. "I finally have time for everything that really matters."

Are you a person with time – time for everything that really matters?

Run hard. Rest well is a ministry designed to encourage people to explore the use of time. Time for work. Time for rest.

Why rest?

Clarity. My friend Kathryn understood, with clarity, the purpose of her life. That understanding brought energy, delight, and focus to her days. These gifts can be ours,

Guilt is a driving force behind much of our exhaustion.

but too often guilt gets in the way. It's a roadblock of monumental proportions. In the devotion from Day 3, I mentioned six roadblocks to rest. Guilt is #7. Guilt routinely dismantles our rest. Guilt routinely blurs our calling, disrupting clarity and focus.

As caring, gifted, responsive people, we are aware of needs and drawn to opportunities. For some of us, the needs of others and the wealth of golden opportunities before us flash like neon lights. Compelled to respond, we end up pulled in many directions, spread too thin, in over our heads.

Can you relate?

Guilt is a driving force behind much of our exhaustion. A remarkable story about guilt is tucked into the very first chapter of Mark. I missed its message for the first 40 years of my life, but it will act as a rudder for the next 40.

Jesus visited Simon's home, where his mother-in-law was sick in bed. Jesus healed her and the news spread quickly (Mark 1:29-38). That evening the whole town gathered at their door. Jesus ministered to each one late into the night. Waking up early the next morning, Jesus slipped away to a quiet place to be alone with His Father. As the sun rose, a fresh batch of people gathered at the house. As long minutes ticked into hours, frustration grew among the people. A group of disciples was sent out to search for Jesus.

This account of Jesus' life reminds us that clarity comes from quiet times off the beaten path.

Rest

When they found Him, they announced, "Everyone is looking for You!" Can you hear their intent to instill guilt? I can.

The people waiting at the house had legitimate needs and a real desire to meet Jesus. Yet listen to Jesus' reply. "Let us go somewhere else..."

What?! Those were real people with real needs and Jesus was going to turn His back on them?
Yes.

As painful as that truth is, Jesus refused to be guilt-driven. Jesus chose, every step of the way, to be Spirit-led. Jesus' holy yes to God's plan for that morning meant an earthly no to real people with real needs.

Were those people disappointed? Yes. Devastated? Likely. Did God leave them out in the cold? No, not for a moment. I do not know how, when or where, but God in all His sovereignty had a plan for their lives – plans to pursue, heal, restore. Maybe that timing was going to unfold three hours later, three months later, or 30 years later. I don't know. But God did. Will I trust Him?

Jesus did.

Why rest? Why slip away to a quiet hillside to watch the sun rise? Why schedule a day with margin in mind? Why take a walk? Why take a break? Because clarity is birthed in calm. This account of Jesus' life reminds

Are you a person with time – time for everything that really matters?

us that clarity comes from quiet times off the beaten path.

This week when a need arises or an opportunity comes knocking on your door, consider these three suggestions:

1. Stop. Refuse to answer on the spot. Reply, "Let me get back to you." Then pray. Listen carefully. If you are living with little margin, any *yes* will demand a *no* to something, whether you want it to or not. What will that be? Face the truth.
2. Know your mission for the season of life you are now living. Name it. Claim it. Be incredibly sensitive and prayerful about any *yes* outside its domain.
3. Following Jesus' lead, remind yourself that saying *yes* or *no* requires direction from the Holy Spirit. It takes conviction, vision and stamina, but it produces joy, confidence and a work of God that far exceeds the guilt-driven *yes* we are inclined to give.

Why rest?

The call of your life depends on it. Mine, too.

There is so much more to explore on this topic, but the first step is about choice. Will I be driven by guilt or led by the Spirit?

Make it Your Own

• Guilt is the gift that keeps on giving or rather, taking – taking chunks out of your joy and heart. How much does guilt play a factor in your life?

• How and when is the Spirit given free rein to sculpt your *yes's* and your *nos.*

Week 1 - Connections

1. Share a high point of this week.

2. Can you list the 4 Rhythms of Rest? Which one comes most naturally? Which one proves most challenging?

3. What did you learn about yourself from the assessment and inventory?

4. Which roadblocks of rest are most distracting?

5. Are you a person with time – time for what matters?

6. Guilt-driven? Spirit-led? How does Mark 1 speak into your life?

Parting Word

Read Jeremiah 2:13.

Allow a minute of silent prayer and reflection or a few minutes for journaling.

Now read Jeremiah 2:23 and 6:16. Read Jeremiah 6:16 one more time, but leave out the last sentence.

Share your thoughts.

Close in a time of prayer.

Pause for Rest

Sleep

Vantage Point | Trek 2

The Default Setting

Stress. I hate that word. It rises up and slaps me in the face. Hard. It reminds me that I am not in control.

I long to face life with grace, grit and determination. Unhindered. Free. But all too often, whether the world sees it or not, the stress of life lands me on my butt.

That's okay. Stress is not actually the enemy. Cortisol is.

Cortisol is a hormone produced in our adrenal glands. Under normal circumstances our body regulates a daily cycle of cortisol. It pumps out the highest levels in the morning to prepare us for the day ahead. It hits a low as we get ready to sleep, preparing our bodies for the sweet land of slumber.

Cortisol is also known as the "stress hormone." Our bodies release an extra dose of cortisol when a tension filled situation arises (a fight-or-flight event). A short-term release of extra cortisol makes a positive impact on the body. It improves memory, reduces our sensitivity to pain and increases energy and stamina. In short, a quick dose of cortisol is a knight in shining armor.

Prolonged overexposure to cortisol, whether it's a constant trickle or a relentless fire hose, is a dragon breathing down our back. The effects singe and destroy.

Our unhealthy habits attempt to alleviate what ails us, but most are short-sighted, causing more pain and loss in the long run.

1. Cortisol damages our brain and does a number on our memory. It sets us up for Alzheimer's.
2. It suppresses our immune system, making us vulnerable to both inconvenient and life-altering illnesses.
3. It plays havoc with our mood, our ability to be patient, self-controlled, and kind.
4. It causes us to gain weight. It increases ghrelin, the hormone that creates the feeling of hunger. It decreases leptin, the hormone that allows us to feel full after eating. Not a good combination.
5. It sets us up for diabetes, depression, high blood pressure and osteoporosis.
6. It sabotages our sleep.
7. It damages the cells in our body and shortens our life span.

> Where do you feel cortisol's greatest effect? Extra pounds? Chronic fatigue? Dwindling joy? Restless nights? Brain cells on strike?

> We all have a *default setting* when it comes to stress and the impact of cortisol over-production.

1. Caffeine – we gulp it down in many ways.
2. Carbs – we crave the temporary "brain boost" we get from our favorite snacks.
3. Pills – we take all kinds for pain, sleep, blood pressure, depression, anxiety (Please do not read between the lines. I thank the Lord for prescription medication. It is a part of God's healing plan. There are times, however, that we'd rather swallow a pill than do the work of health and healing.)
4. Ruts – we cave, allowing unhealthy routines and habits to form, mini vices that provide a quick fix.
5. Moods – we rant and rave, pout and complain.

> We all have our default setting – our personal set of unhealthy (and healthy) habits to

Sleep

deal with the barrage of daily strain and demands. Our unhealthy habits attempt to alleviate what ails us, but most are short-sighted, causing more pain and loss in the long run.

Make it Your Own

• Where do you feel cortisol's greatest effect?

• What's your default setting? Does Romans 7:15 NIV ring true? *I do not understand what I do. For what I want to do, I do not do, but what I hate I do.*

• What was your default setting five years ago? Ten years ago? What would you like to change about it?

• Pray. Not to be changed. But to see clearly/truthfully. And to be open to the process of change God wants to initiate.

Game Plan

Stress is not our enemy. Stress is good, healthy and necessary. The culprit is cortisol and our inability to recognize when there's too much. It is the masked bandit that robs us of more than we can imagine.

Here are some surprisingly easy, stress-free, healthy strategies for dealing with too much cortisol.

1. **Breathe.** Americans are famous for shallow, anemic breathing. Just a few, slow, deep breaths trigger the vagus nerve – every time. This signals the nervous system to lower the heart rate, which in turn helps the body recover from an overdose of cortisol. Tape up sticky notes that say *"Breathe!"* or set a timer on your cell phone. Bedtime and red lights are great places to practice. Experts tell us there's an art to breathing well. Begin by exhaling out through your mouth. Then take a slow breath in through your nose. Don't go too slow or too fast. Breathe at a normal rate, just make it sure it's deep. At the height of your deep breath, pause for a second of two. Try to use your abdominal muscles and if you're sitting upright, don't allow your shoulders to rise. Make sure they are relaxed. Five to ten deep breaths will serve you well.

2. **Hydrate.** Mild dehydration adds to our fatigue and crankiness. Drink some water. Then a little bit more. Most Americans suffer from mild levels of dehydration every day. Don't like to drink? Use a straw. A quick sip from a straw gets more in you then a sip from a cup.

3. **Hold and hug.** Wrap your arms around some people you love. Every day. Human touch reduces cortisol levels (Sumioka, Nakae, Kanai, & Ishiguro, 2013). It's life-giving to premature babies and just about everyone else. Kissing

works, too!

4. **Linger outside.** Meander to your car. Most Americans spend only 14 minutes outside every day – an accumulation of the short bursts we spend walking from a building to our car and back again. This cortisol reducer simply encourages us to pause and pay attention. Feel the breeze, the rain, the sunshine. Listen for birds. Notice the clouds, a splash of color, the dance of leaves or branches in the wind. Attend. Then take a moment to marvel. If you see a rose, you know what to do.

5. **Smile.** Simply smile. (Laugh, too, every chance you get.) A genuine smile reduces your heart rate even in stressful, multi-tasking situations. Go figure. So, shine those pearly whites at every person you meet. If they're under five, add a wink free of charge.

6. **Thank the Lord.** Every night. Three things. Be specific. Ann Voskamp (2011) encourages us to make a list of a thousand things we're thankful for. A year of gratitude goes a long way. Begin tonight. Better yet, begin right now.

Have you ever tried changing your *default setting*? Make a game plan.
Give it a try. Don't give up.

Breathe. Drink. Hug. Attend. Smile. Say thank you.

Big steps in the right direction.

Make it Your Own

• What simple cortisol-busters are most attractive to you?

Sleep

We cannot circumvent many of the stressors in our lives: looming deadlines, cranky babies, debt, troubled teens, medical mayhem. (A magic wand about right now would be really nice.) But we can minimize the damage of 24/7 cortisol. Two steps are required:

1. What are the objective realities of too much cortisol in your body?

    Are you a grouch?

    Do you have trouble falling or staying asleep?

    Are you gaining unwanted weight or can't take off what you'd like to lose?

    Is your doctor concerned about your blood pressure, cholesterol or blood sugar?

    Are you frequently ill or fighting an autoimmune disease?

    Is joy a missing ingredient in the equation of life?
2. Name it. Claim it. And face the enemy. Cortisol.

Diminishing the cortisol overload in our body will diminish these ugly, objective realities. Is it the only answer? No. But it packs a powerful punch. Let's begin with sleep. We'll explore a few additional cortisol-busting possibilities in the devotion from Day 8.

Sleep

Cortisol wreaks havoc on our sleep. Sixty percent of Americans wrestle with insomnia occasionally or regularly (National Sleep Foundation, 2011).

Does the shoe fit? The lack of sleep is devastating. People who get less than six hours of sleep at night have a 50% increase of cortisol the next day (Leproult, Copinschi, Buxton, & Van Cauter, 1977). Working *hard* at getting seven to eight restorative hours of sleep most nights will place you light-years ahead on the road to rest and restoration.

This devotional thought is not going to go into the "how-tos" of good sleep. That information is out there for you to explore. You may even need to visit your doctor, especially if it's a chronic issue or there is any concern of sleep apnea. Don't brush it off. Give it the attention it deserves. Please.

The goal of this chapter is for you to see the value of sleep. It is likely *the* most important thing you can do to reduce the damaging effects of cortisol overload in your life. If you live with little margin, taking the time to sleep is one of the most productive things you can do. It is not a waste of time as some are inclined to believe.

Prioritize sleep – for you and everyone in your family. Check out this article from *Reader's Digest*, March 2015 (http://www.rd.com/health/conditions/america-sleep-crisis/).

Want to get a good night's sleep? Here are some surprising tips.

- Wear socks.
- Go screen-free for 60-120 minutes before bed. The blue light waves dismantle the melatonin your brain is trying to pump out to prepare your body for a good night's sleep (Figueiro, Wood, Plitnick, & Rea, 2011). If you must be

looking at a screen (any size), consider buying some nifty blue light shades. They are orange in color and work.

- If you find yourself waking up in the middle of the night, try eating some protein before going to sleep. If blood sugar falls too low at night, our adrenal glands pump out a little adrenaline in an attempt to wake you up … to eat (even if you don't feel hungry.)
- Create a new sleep routine for Fido … that does not include your bed. Pet owners who sleep with their furry buddies lose more shut-eye than they may realize.
- Do a med check! Taking certain medications in the evening may set you up for insomnia. Beta blockers are one such medication. Investigate!
- Sleep apnea. Get it checked out. Don't delay. It can take years off your life.
- Increase your body's GABA reception. Consider trying L-Theanine 200 mg and/or chamomile tea each evening.
- Concerned about your children's moodiness, weight gain, school performance? Make sure they get 8 to 10 hours of sleep.

Make it Your Own

• What value does sleep hold in your life? Do you prioritize it? Neglect it? Fight it?

• If you were able to read the *Reader's Digest* article on sleep from March 2015, what did you learn?

Definition of Sanity

The *definition of insanity* has played a part in altering the choices I make in my life on a number of occasions. Have you ever heard it?

The definition of insanity is *"doing what you've always done, but expecting different results"* (The Basic Text of Narcotics Anonymous,1992, p. 11). Have you ever fallen prey? I am indebted for the insight of this definition. It's given me pause more than once – especially in the arena of cortisol overload.

Getting seven to nine hours of sleep each night is a game changer, but there are other commitments that can usher in a new measure of sanity into your life. The first list only requires minutes of your time. The second requires a greater investment of time. The third is a list we need to seriously consider. Nothing hard here, just rich rewards.

Do you know that our bodies are chemical factories? All of these cortisol-busting suggestions have solid science behind them. Each one plays a role in enhancing our body's ability to pump out calming hormones or slow down the outpouring of cortisol and adrenaline. Give them a try.

Working hard to get 7 to 8 hours of restorative hours of sleep most nights will place you light years ahead on the road to rest and restoration.

List #1

1. Take five. Go outside intentionally. Five, simple, quiet minutes outside enhanced the well-being of people fighting depression, across the board. It was an astounding finding.

Set a timer. Go. Step outside. Look for the moon. Watch a bird or a bug. Listen to the wind. You won't be disappointed. Every day – eight weeks.

2. Give yourself a bedtime – for one week. If you're a guy, start the process 10 minutes ahead of time. If you're a woman, make it an hour. Assess and repeat. Seven extra hours of sleep each week will give you the equivalent of one extra night of sleep. You may end up feeling like a million bucks.

3. Drink all the caffeine you want – before 1 pm.

4. Make sure all your snacks have some protein. If a snack is all carbs, the sugar slump will lay you low. (The same rule applies to meals, especially breakfast.)

5. Take a 10-20 minute power nap. Do some deep breathing while you're at it.

6. Daniel prayed three times a day. Do a Daniel. We too easily forget that God is near, attentive, Almighty, compassionate. His Presence makes a difference.

7. Cuddle. The warmth of sustained contact puts us on the fast-track of cortisol reduction.

8. Read the *Serenity Prayer* twice every day. "God grant me the serenity to accept the things I cannot change; courage to change the things I can; and wisdom to know the difference." (Niebuhr, n.d.)

9. Evenings. Create and guard quiet nights at home. Mark them on your calendar. Feel no guilt when something else surfaces. Simply reply, "I'm sorry, I have a prior commitment – to *sanity*!"

List # 2

1. Learn the art of massage. Back rubs. Give them. Receive them. Hands. Feet. Ears. Scalp. Face. Touch is a powerful thing.

2. Are you discouraged by how little you get done each day? That fact increases cortisol production. Chunk your time in order to tackle a project. Allow no digital distraction. No e-mail. No phone calls. No Facebook. No Twitter. Some larger engineering companies recognized that productivity was waning among workers, yet hours-on-the-job was increasing. Mandatory "silent/no-tech" times upped productivity and lowered work hours. Give it a try.

3. We were made for community. Many of us are lonely. Reach out. Join a home Bible study. Invite an old friend to lunch.

4. Are you carrying a heavy load of past hurts? Do what you need to do to set healing into motion. Unhealed wounds fester. The cortisol damage is insidious. Go to AA. Find a counselor. Check out a Christian 12-Step program. We weren't meant to go at it alone. Ever.

List #3

1. We were made to move. Exercising 20-30 minutes most days is a tremendous reducer of cortisol. Tremendous! Walking is a great place to start. Don't have 30 minutes? Walk for 10 minutes in the morning and 10 minutes in the evening. Invite God to join you. He's been known to do that (Genesis 3:8).

2. Has exercise lagged behind as one of the last things on your "to do" list? It's been that way for me, especially while we were raising our kids. It was a luxury of time I did not think I had. We've known from years that exercise is good for the body, but there is a truck load of evidence saying that it's even better for the brain. It may very well be THE best thing we can do to stay emotionally healthy and cognitively sharp. This New York Times Magazine article by Gretchen Reynolds (2012) is absolutely outstanding. Enjoy! http://

www.nytimes.com/2012/04/22/magazine/how-exercise-could-lead-to-a-better-brain.html?_r=0

3. If time allows, check out this comprehensive article from the Center for Disease Control (2015) article on the benefits of moving your body. The list is pretty staggering. http://www.cdc.gov/physicalactivity/everyone/health/index.html

Make it Your Own

• Take a look at all three lists. Choose a cortisol-buster and pursue it. Tell a friend. Invite them to keep you accountable. Shoot for 21 days. Experts tell us that a good three-week stint may set into motion the blessings of a new good habit.

Week 2 - Connections

1. What does cortisol overload look like in your body? What negative effect concerns you the most?

2. Sleep? Do you get enough? Is it restorative?

3. Are you willing to prioritize it?
What would you have to start doing or stop doing to make sleep a priority?

4.Which of the cortisol-busting possibilities are most attractive and inviting?

5. Write them out. Tape it to your bathroom mirror.
Invite your family and friends to join you.

6. Share a success story. How, when or where did you enjoy the simple blessings of a cortisol-busting activity this week?

Parting Word

Read Proverbs 17:22 and Psalm 3:5 / 4:8.

Allow a minute of silent prayer and reflection **or** a few minutes for journaling.

Read Proverbs 17:22 and Psalm 3:5 / 4:8 again.

Share your thoughts.

Close in a time of prayer.

3 Sabbath Keeping
Vantage Point | Trek 3

50

Near and Dear

God says, "*Remember* the Sabbath."
I forget.
I forget a lot.
Even though this commandment gets little attention, it's an easy one to "keep" by most standards: go to church.
Sixty minutes later, our duty is done, our Sabbath is kept.
Most of us don't even know what we're missing.
To combat my propensity for forgetfulness, I've discovered some insights that help me remember: truth, confession and a white flag.

Truth

A peek into God's Word gives us a peek into God's heart.
Last words carry some weight, some clout. When Moses came off of Mt. Sinai (the first time) after his 40-day encounter with the Living God, take note of God's final instructions to Moses:

Then the Lord said to Moses, "Say to the Israelites, 'You must observe My Sabbaths. This will be a sign between Me and you for the generations to come, so you may know that I am the Lord, who makes you holy ... For six days work is to be done, but the seventh day is a day of Sabbath rest, holy to the Lord. Whoever does any work on the Sabbath day is to be put to death. The Israelites are to observe the Sabbath, celebrating it for the generations to come as

A peek into God's Word gives us a peek into God's heart.

a lasting covenant. It will be a sign between Me and the Israelites forever, for in six days the Lord made the heavens and the earth, and on the seventh day He rested and was refreshed.'"
Exodus 31:12-13, 15-17 NIV

Remember that *Sabbath Keeping* is Commandment #4*. It's found in Exodus 20 and Deuteronomy 5. The first three commandments speak about our relationship with God. The final six speak about our relationship with people. Number four is the bridge. Sabbath Keeping impacts our walk with God *and* our walk with each other. My children will attest to this fact. Mama is a whole lot easier to live with when she's rested and refreshed.

When it comes to Sabbath Keeping, God pulled out His highlighter. More than once. He added exclamation points in all five books of the Torah and throughout the entire Old Testament. Outside of idolatry, this commandment is near and dear to the heart of God. It shows up all over the place. Moses seemed to get the point. First chance he got, coming off Mt. Sinai (the second time), Moses shared what was most pressing on God's agenda and his. (The first time Moses came down, he ran smack dab into an idolatry-fest.)

Moses assembled the whole Israelite community and said to them, "These are the things the Lord has commanded you to do: For six days, work is to be done, but the

Sabbath

seventh day shall be your holy day, a Sabbath
of rest to the Lord ..."
Exodus 35:1-2a NIV

The truth is – God takes Sabbath quite
seriously.
Where does Sabbath fall on God's priority
list?
Where does it fall on mine?
Don't jump ahead to the "How in the world
would this work?" Just focus on the Word.
Allow the Spirit free and full rein.

*When most Christians number the Ten
Commandments, Sabbath Keeping comes
up #4. Lutheran and Catholic believers
recognize it as #3. This happens because
they combine Commandments 1 and 2 and
divide #10 into two parts.

Make it Your Own

• What did Sabbath Keeping look like when you were growing up?

• What does it look like in your life today?

• Have you ever been taught how to keep the Sabbath holy ... wholly? Has anyone modeled a pace of life that includes a distinct, set-apart time for rest?

• Have you ever felt convicted about the priority and practice of Sabbath Keeping in your life?

Holy Ground

Confession

When it comes to embracing the rhythm and rest of Sabbath Keeping, conviction is likely the first step, but the next step is always confession. It's where the rubber meets the road. Confession means agreeing with God. It's a simple, powerful, God-directed interior redesign. We make it hard, however.

> **Confession means agreeing with God. It's a simple, powerful, God directed interior redesign.**

When we are confronted by the fact that we fall short of God's best, we often sidetrack confession. Instead of starting on our knees, we make a plan for making things better. Feeling convicted and guilty, we want to right the wrong. We want to save face. Amend our ways. As followers of Jesus, we are not really accustomed to grace. It makes us squirm. We talk about it, but we try to live without it.

The Prodigal Son did just that. Hungry, gaunt and broken, he recognized he made a wrong turn. Instead of simply walking home to where he belonged, he made a plan (Luke 15). "I'll work for my father. I'll feed the pigs. Surely he'll comply." We like to be in control, especially when we come up broke, with egg on our face.

When I was first convicted of my nine-commandment form of following Jesus, I bypassed confession and moved right into rectification. I was going to make things right – do Sabbath the way it should be done. Boom. Bang. All set. Case closed.

I moved into my Sabbath Keeping with conviction, but also confusion and loads of disappointment. There are a number of reasons why my first 108 weeks of remembering the Sabbath (two years' worth!) were miserable, but a critical first misstep was bypassing confession. I failed to fall on my knees. Instead I justified, blamed and planned.

By God's grace I've learned (in the arena of Sabbath Keeping and many other arenas) that when conviction sets in, I need to name my sin and claim it. Nothing more. Nothing less.

When it's an issue that has a vise-grip on my heart, I need to share it with another person. I need to say it out loud. There is something powerful about an out-loud confession. James 5:16 NIV nails it:
Therefore confess your sins to each other and pray for each other so that you may be healed.

Confession releases the power of God into my transformation. An out-loud confession invites me to be honest. It's painful. It lays me low. It's a place of vulnerability and deep surrender but it is life-giving.

God meets me, arms opened wide. He pulls me into an embrace on His terms, not mine. The generosity and extravagance of God's love redefines me, the moment, and my future.

Is the Lord shining a light on your Sabbath

It's a place of vulnerability and deep surrender but it is life-giving.

Keeping? Does He want something more for you through it? Does He want something more for Himself because of it? Like a chunk of your heart and the focus of your affection?

When the time is right, find the prayer in Daniel 9:4-19 and make it your own. Don't measure your ability or desire to change your ways. This moment is not about the future. It's about meeting God with the white flag flying. Come empty-handed – recognizing and confessing that you have forgotten to remember, honor, delight, in a day God made for you and Him to enjoy together. This is where the rubber meets the road. When it does, you'll find yourself standing on Holy Ground.

Make it Your Own

• Where is the Prodigal alive and well within your soul?

• What are you going to do about it? Daniel 9:4-19 might be a good place to start.

• The power of this week's theme is not in the words I've shared, but what you and God will do behind closed doors or out in the open with a very close friend. Knee pads are recommended, but not required.

White Flags

Sabbath Keeping.
The work of *surrender* is mine – surrendering up the hours of my days each week.
The work of *transformation* is God's.
No doubt about it.

We find this promise of God's workmanship in our lives in Ezekiel 36.

Rest is not an all-or-nothing deal. Rest is blessed, no matter the amount.

> *I will give you a new heart and put a new spirit in you; I will remove from you your heart of stone and give you a heart of flesh. And I will put My Spirit in you and move you to follow My decrees and be careful to keep my laws. This is what the Sovereign Lord says: On the day I cleanse you from all your sins, I will resettle your towns, and the ruins will be rebuilt. The desolate land will be cultivated instead of lying desolate in the sight of all who pass through it. They will say, "This land that was laid waste has become like the Garden of Eden; the cities that were lying in ruins, desolate and destroyed, are now fortified and inhabited. Then the nations around you that remain will know that I the Lord have rebuilt what was destroyed and have replanted what was desolate. I the Lord have spoken, and I will do it.*
> Ezekiel 36:26-27, 33-36 NIV

The promise is trustworthy.
The transformation will be visible.
Our lives will be rebuilt, cultivated, fortified, replanted.

But where do we begin? For me, it began
with pondering this question.
*If God says I can accomplish my work in six days,
who am I to say I can't?*
I had to learn to honor the work that got
done each week and trust God with all that
didn't. We rest because God says to do it,
not because we have completed our work.

1. The Sabbath is designed to be anticipated. The day before
   our Sabbath is an important day*. It takes forethought. It
   demands discernment between the tasks that are a *must do*
   and the tasks that are a *like to do*. When our Sabbath Rest
   is upon us, we have an opportunity to *lay down* what did
   not get done and *lift up* (as a gift of thanksgiving) what did.
   This moment of surrender unlocks the door for me to be
   refreshed by the rest God has waiting for me to enjoy.   *I
   respect Saturday Sabbath Keepers, but I also respect
   Sunday Sabbath Keepers. (In the early church, Sunday was
   called the Lord's Day: Acts 20:4, I Cor. 16:2, Rev. 1:10.) I
   respect those who reserve any given day of the week as their
   Sabbath day of Rest. I believe God is honored when we
   follow the seven-day cycle He established.
2. As we begin to explore Sabbath Keeping through a biblical
   world view, 24 hours may feel unrealistic. Some of us are
   familiar with rest. Some of us have forgotten what it's like.
   If you are new to rest, go easy on yourself. Committing
   to "shorter blocks" of time may allow you to keep the
   momentum going without becoming discouraged and
   throwing in the towel. I don't know what God would say
   about this, but taking a "shorter block" was a plan that
   initially worked for me as I reoriented my life. I took baby
   steps before being able to fully embrace the 24-hour gift
   full-tilt.

Rest is not an all-or-nothing deal.
Rest is blessed, no matter the amount.

This week, when will your Sabbath Rest take place? Can you set aside 24 hours, eight hours, two hours? For those who must work seven days each week, can you set aside three portions of time? A morning here. An evening there. And one afternoon over there? However you begin, begin. That's the key. Then savor the gift –guilt-free.

Make it Your Own

Surrender plays a major role when it comes to embracing the gift of Sabbath Rest.
White flags are easy to come by, but hard to raise.
Do you have the strength it takes?
Don't worry, God does.

> "...He who began a good work in you will carry it on to completion." Philippians 1:6 NIV

Close by reading Ezekiel 36:25-38 in its entirety.

On Your Honor

What does Sabbath Rest look like in the 21st century?
It has a lot to do with honor. Three things come to mind when it comes to honoring the Sabbath.

#1 Honor its Maker

Recognize that the Sabbath is a day made *by* God, *for* God and given *to* us as a means to remember who He is and who we are.
It is a day with a singular purpose – to rest well in the company of God and those we love so that we are recharged, refreshed and refueled for the week ahead (Exodus 23:12).

Leviticus 23:1-3 reminds us that group worship is a part of Sabbath Keeping, but it's not the only ingredient God uses to refresh our souls.

How are *you* best refreshed by God?
Do you know?

Feel free to think inside the box:
Is it personal quiet time? Large group worship? Quiet walks? In-depth Bible study? Music? Praying with a friend?

Feel free to think outside the box:
What might that be?
Dancing? Rock climbing? Singing?
Canoeing? Drawing? Fishing? Kite flying?
An extended time of prayer?
The sky is the limit. So are the blessings of meeting with God on a day

set apart for Him.

Sabbath Keeping in the 21st century begins with honoring the Commandment and its Creator. Allow creativity full rein.

#2 Honor Yourself

Are you familiar with activities that are delightful *and* restorative? It's a powerful combination. Most of us know what we enjoy, but sometimes those activities aren't necessarily restorative. Experiment. Try out some activities that are both enjoyable and restorative. Not sure where to begin?

Ask yourself, "What do I *need*?" or "Where am I running on the fumes of an empty tank?" If you're part of a family and you sense a collective need ask, "What do *we* need?"

After living through this past week, does one particular need rise above the others? Are you feeling physically depleted? Spiritually dry? Emotionally empty? Relationally weary or wanting? Don't gloss over this list. Ask yourself these questions. It's an important place to begin.

Then prioritize those needs as much as possible. Some of us are facing overwhelming challenges that have us in over-our-heads. Sabbath Keeping during these intense seasons of life
must be sculpted by a level of immense creativity and commitment. It gives the word *challenging* new meaning, but it is possible.

Top Picks to Consider:
1. **Sleep**. Prioritize it. Enjoy it. Feel no guilt.
2. **Do what delights you**. Find pleasure in simple things.
3. **Unplug**.
4. **Tag team.** If you have small children, two-hour blocks work great.
5. **Don't cook**. I don't, but please, please do if it's a source of joy and delight.
6. **Get outside**. Make it a priority.
7. **FFF** – "Forced" family fun may not work. It never did for us, especially as the kids got older. Simple, fun traditions were enjoyed by all. Roasting mini-marshmallows with toothpicks over candles. Ice cream and popcorn for Sunday supper. A Sunday stroll.
8. **Enjoy the people you love**. Laugh out loud.
9. **Enjoy the Presence of God**. On a walk, in a closet, through your worship, with a friend, on your knees, by a stream, in the Word.

Allow your heart free rein to dream. Then
set a course.

#3 Honor Others

We are a generation with neither model,
method nor mentors in the arena of Sabbath
Rest. It's foreign territory – mysterious and
unexplored. Be a pioneer. Take the path
less traveled. Place a priority and create an
atmosphere in your home where Sabbath
Rest is welcomed and honored
as a day of devotion and delight.
Others will take note.

Your weekly commitment to a rhythm of
work and rest might be what God uses to
ignite a hunger in others for this rhythm
made in heaven.

Our job this week? *Run hard* – break a sweat, stay focused, give it all you've got, but set apart some time to put your feet up. Let out that deep sigh and rest. *Rest well.* Fully. Deeply. Guilt-free.

Make it Your Own

What might a rhythm of Sabbath Keeping look like for you in this season of your life?

This week, what do you need most from your Sabbath Rest?

Who in your sphere of influence might discover the remarkable rewards of Sabbath Rest as they watch rhythm unfold in your life?

Week 3 - Connections

1. Sabbath starts with command and moves to conviction and confession. Where are you finding yourself on this journey? Have you found knee pads or white flags helpful?

2. How easy or hard is it to recognize that the Sabbath is a day made *by* God, *for* God and given *to* us as a means to remember who He is and who we are?

3. As you take the path less traveled, who will you invite or encourage to join you along the way? What does this mean? What does this look like?

4. Are you ready to re-orient the basic pattern and rhythm of your life? What's the first step? What might your day (or hours of) Sabbath Rest look like this week?

Parting Word

Read Isaiah 58:11-14

      Allow a minute of silent prayer and reflection **or** a few minutes for journaling.

Read Isaiah 58:11-14 again.

Share your thoughts.

Close in a time of prayer.

4 *Stillness*
Vantage Point | Trek 4

Dare to Dialogue

Prayer.

If I'm really honest, I have to admit I find it easier to spend ten minutes talking *about* God than ten minutes talking *to* God. My life bears evidence of this reality too often. My growth can be meager. My fruit is nothing worth writing home about.

Can you relate?

How do we turn the tide? How do we infuse our lives, our passion, our purpose, our existence with prayer – so our lives find the rest and power we long for? I think the first step is examining our understanding and practice of prayer. For 40 years, a majority of my prayer life has been spent in monologue. I talk. God listens. Nothing wrong with talking. God wants to hear from His children. But it can't consume. Monologue does not set me on the fast track to a healthy relationship with anyone, including God.

Does a prayer monologue come easier than dialogue to you, too? Getting a glimpse of Moses' relationship with God spurs me on to explore this whole idea of dialogue. I think the whole idea of *dialogue* prayer captured Joshua's
heart as well.

Now Moses used to take a tent and pitch it outside the camp some distance away, calling it the "tent of meeting." Anyone inquiring of the Lord would go to the tent

I have to admit I find it easier to spend ten minutes talking about God than ten minutes talking to God.

> **Monologue does not set me on the fast track to a healthy relationship with anyone, including God.**

of meeting outside the camp. ... **The Lord would speak to Moses** *face to face, as a man speaks with his friend. Then Moses would return to the camp, but his young aid Joshua son of Nun did not leave the tent.* Exodus 33:7 and 11 NIV

Face to face with God.
Start tomorrow morning.
Start right now.

Give ears to my words, O Lord, consider my sighing. Listen to my cry for help, my King and my God, for to You I pray. Morning by morning, O Lord, You hear my voice; morning by morning I lay my requests before You and wait in expectation. Psalm 5:1-3 NIV

Make it Your Own

Who taught you to pray? How did they teach you to pray? Do you have children? How have you taught them how to pray?

How does prayer give shape to your priorities, your purpose, your peace?

God Speaks

God speaks to us through creation.
He speaks to us through His Word.
He speaks to quiet hearts. (Busy hearts, too,
but the reception can be fuzzy.)

When I was little, I was baffled – *baffled* – by
Jesus' desire to pray. "Why would Jesus want
to pray?" Prayer was about getting stuff.
"He was God," I reasoned. "Jesus didn't
need anything."

Jesus *needed* nothing. Jesus *desired* the
presence of His Father.

Do you think he was homesick? Maybe.
Am I ever homesick? Do I ever long for the
presence of my Father?

Over the years, prayer for me has moved
(and is moving) from *getting things* to *getting
God*.

Part of that journey includes dialogue –
embracing a relational attitude to prayer.
It's about learning to listen to God, not only
in His Word (which is primary), but how to
listen to God in stillness.

For me, listening to God in prayer is
attending to His Presence. It is being still. It
is knowing He is present. It is entering into
a stillness that is quiet enough to hear His
heartbeat and His song. It is where I feel
most deeply loved.

> **Jesus needed nothing. Jesus desired the presence of His Father.**

Zephaniah 3:17 NIV rises up to spotlight this truth.

> *The Lord your God is with you; He is mighty to save. He will take great delight in you, He will quiet you with His love, He will rejoice over you with singing.**

Stillness reminds me I occupy a treasured place in the heart of God. This promise is found in Psalm 46:10a NIV.

> *Be still, and know that I am God.*

In stillness, God reveals Himself to me. I cannot *see* God. I cannot *hear* God. I cannot *feel* God.

But I can *know* God. And in knowing God, He assures me of my identity, directs my footsteps and shapes my heart's desires.

* For the warriors among us, take a look at this verse in the *Holman Christian Standard Bible*. Nashville: Broadman & Holman, 2003:

> *Yahweh your God is among you, a warrior who saves. He will rejoice over you with gladness. He will bring you quietness with His love. He will delight in you with shouts of joy.* Zephaniah 3:17

Do I ever long for the presence of my Father?

Make it Your Own

What does it mean in your life to experience the Presence of God?

Think about this past week. Did you experience the Presence of God?

This can be a difficult question. That's OK. No shame or blame. Reflect. This kind of question invites a response.

Knowing God

Be still, and know that I am God...
Psalm 46:10a(NIV)
Two scriptural accounts have formed my *knowing* God.

Satisfied

But I have stilled and quieted my soul;
like a weaned child with its mother, like a
weaned child is my soul within me.
Psalm 131:2 NIV

This stillness and quiet, this "knowing" God, places me on Holy Ground.

While growing up, a picture of God's loving care that captured my heart was a nursing mother with her child (Isaiah 66:11). It still does, but now my "priceless" picture of God's love is that of a weaned child with his mother. A weaned child does not want anything from mom. He is in her arms content and fully satisfied. All he wants and needs is her presence.

When I am *still* in the Presence of God, when I attend to Him in prayer, when my quieted heart listens for His heartbeat, I find the source of my satisfaction – the Presence of God. This stillness and quiet, this "knowing" God, places me on Holy Ground.

Attentive

An account in the book of Joshua points us to an active stance of "knowing" God. It speaks to us of Holy Ground (Joshua 5:13-15 NIV). In it, Joshua encounters an angel, a commander in the army of God. Joshua falls face down, humbled and in awe. "*What*

message does my Lord have for His servant?"
Upon hearing that question, the angel announces, *"Take off your sandals, for the place you are standing is holy."*

Meeting with God is a holy thing. All too often I enter my prayer time distracted and in haste, with a casualness that leads to callousness. I want to replace my casualness and callousness with attentiveness and awe.

"What message does my Lord have for His servant?"

What message does He have for me? Am I familiar with His voice?

...the sheep listen for His (the Shepherd's) voice. He calls His own sheep by name and leads them out. When He has brought out all His own, He goes on ahead of them, and His sheep follow Him because they know His voice.
John 10:3b-4 NIV

**"What message does my Lord have for His servant?"
Joshua 5:14**

Make it Your Own

What does "stillness" mean to you? What does it look like? What does it feel like?

How often in your prayer life do you feel satisfied?

How often in your prayer life do you feel attentive?

P. R. A. Y.

Find rest, O my soul, in God alone. Psalm 62:5a
NIV
This promise speaks to me of prayer.
The word P.R.A.Y. is a helpful tool for me as
I explore ways to find rest for my soul.

P – Pause

A momentary halt. Even though my
intentional time with God happens early
in the morning, my mind is already racing,
running full steam ahead. Stillness involves
a quieted heart. The word *pause* helps me
acknowledge the holy reverence of coming
before the Throne of the mighty, creative,
passionate God of all the universe. I pause,
recognizing His Presence.

R – Rejoice

Gratitude alters a relationship. Entitlement
is ugly. Taking time to recognize God's
goodness is a gift to me, and a gift to God.
Sometimes I sing. Sometimes I reflect on the
names and character of God. Sometimes
I share with Him a very specific list of
overdue, heartfelt "thank yous."

A – Attend

This is where I choose to be intentionally
still. I recognize that I am homesick.
Hungry. Longing. My soul finds a resting
place. I acknowledge the mystery and
miracle of stillness. I don't have to fully
understand it. Many days I find a deep
satisfaction in the Presence of God. Some
days I'm too flighty, too distracted or too

> **Gratitude alters a relationship. Entitlement is ugly.**

rushed. Intentional stillness prepares my heart to be more attentive, more watchful of His Presence in the moment, as well as the rest of the day. Sometimes this *quiet time* lasts for seconds, sometimes minutes. Sometimes I ask, *"What message does my Lord have for His servant?"* (Joshua 5:14c NIV). As I attend to the Presence of God through stillness, I rest well and learn how to listen.

Y – Yield

Here I dig into God's Word. As I listen closely to what He has to say, I yield to His Truth. I pay attention to who He is and all that He has to tell me. I have a passionate hunger for the words of God. It's been a lifelong journey. In regard to studying God's Word, someone once challenged me to "Go slow. Live it. Pray it through." Too often in my zeal, I read too much. There is power in keeping it short, going slow, and allowing time for inventory and meditation. When I do that, His Word is more inclined to sink deeply into my soul and not run off a hardened heart.

Psalm 46:10 is a favorite, but we must take the time to read the whole verse, the whole psalm. Too often we stop short.

> *Be still, and know that I am God. I will be exalted among the nations. I will be exalted in the earth.* Psalm 46:10 NIV

The *exaltation* of God. Is the exaltation of God linked to my ability to *be still and know?*

Make it Your Own

Spend some time in Psalm 46.

Will you find P.R.A.Y. a helpful tool to use as you pray?

Is the exaltation of God linked to my ability to *be still and know*?

Week 4 - Connections

1. What have you learned about "being still?" What opens the door to stillness in your life?

2. Does your prayer life include "dialogue" with God?

3. Do you think Jesus was "homesick?" Does your "homesickness" propel you into the arms of God or away? Through it, how does God make Himself known to you?

4. What does satisfaction look like in your life? What does attentiveness look like?

Parting Word

Read Genesis 16:7-13. (Read verses 1-6 if you're not familiar with this story.)

Allow a minute of silent prayer and reflection.
Read verse 8.
Has God asked you any questions lately?
If not, what's a question He might throw your direction?

Read Genesis 16:13 again.

Share your thoughts.

Close in a time of prayer.

Pause for Stillness

5 Solitude

Vantage Point | Trek 1

80

Retreat!

"Retreat!"
It's a *battle cry* of the beloved.
It's strategic.
It is revolutionary.

My first personal retreat was an open door that welcomed my heart back home to rest. As a deeply ingrained over-extender, the power of personal retreat was eye-opening and heart-softening. Regular getaways with God have drastically and beautifully altered the course of my life. Retreat takes the best of all four biblical rhythms of rest (Sabbath, Sleep, Stillness, and Solitude) and wraps them up in a few quiet hours off the beaten path.

But we resist.
We don't have time.
Satan pulls out every lie, trick and detour.
He is desperate to keep us from such treasure.

E. M. Bounds (2009) reminds us: *A holy life does not live in the closet, but it cannot live without it.*

Yet, a commitment to personal retreat does not dwell in the priorities of our hearts or minds. We assign it to a place of insignificance. We see it as an activity for the spiritually elite, the recluse or those with too much time
on their hands. We are unaware that it has profound power to refuel and refresh those on the front lines. Truth be told, "retreat"

> **Retreat! Is the battle cry of those longing to advance the Kingdom of God**

is a battle-cry for those longing to see the Kingdom of God advance, bringing light and hope to dark places and lonely hearts.

It begins with our own.

There are three kinds of personal retreats: offensive, defensive and forced.

Offensive

Jesus was the poster child for *offensive* retreats. Time away with His Father was planned, prioritized, and routine. He recognized the importance of getting away. Jesus was known to "head for the hills." Take a look at the book of Luke in the New Testament. Start with 5:15. Then visit 4:1, 14 and 42. Finish up with 6:12-13, 9:18, 11:1 and 22:39. Jesus was a man of retreat.

Defensive

The story of John the Baptist's beheading speaks to us of our need for *defensive* personal retreats. Matthew 14:13 tells us that when Jesus received the devastating news of His cousin's death, He withdrew from the hubbub, taking a boat by Himself to a solitary place. Although we don't know what Jesus was feeling, I think it's safe to make some guesses. Jesus' heart was heavy. He was sad, angry, aching. He desired to get away. He needed focused time with His Father.
Ever felt that way? Don't resist the urge to pull away.

Jesus was a man of retreat

Don't resist the need to pull away

Forced

Jonah's three-day stint in the belly of a large fish is probably one of the most unique personal retreats in the history of the world. Can't quite imagine the stink and the slime. Not too many travel brochures on that destination. Truth is – God likes to whisper, but if He can't get our attention, He's been known to throw a brick. I'll take a whisper over a brick any day, but a *forced* personal retreat is a tactic God uses to grab our attention.

It's grabbed mine.

"Retreat!"

Will you choose an *offensive* retreat in the next six weeks?
Get your red pen. Pick a day or a half a day. Even two quiet hours off the beaten path will do.

"Retreat!" It is the battle cry of those longing to advance the Kingdom of God.

God likes to whisper, but if he can't get your attention he may throw a brick

Make it Your Own

Do you know anyone committed to personal retreat?

Have you ever engaged? Why? Why not?

What might be your biggest obstacle? Make it a matter of prayer.

Dacha

Dacha is one of my favorite words. It's Russian and I was introduced to it in the town of Istra, Russia in January 2012 while speaking on the topic of rest and retreat at a conference for Christian camp leaders. *Dacha* is a "getaway" cottage – a place of retreat. The use of this word makes Russian faces light up and eyes dance with joy.

What word makes your eyes dance? What word lightens your load? I pray it might become the word *retreat*.

Allow retreat to become an intentional rhythm, priority in your life

Here are a few things I've learned:

1. Retreat is the pursuit of God off the beaten path. It can take place in a single, solitary hour. Or it can span many hours, many days. Many miss the glorious gift of retreat because they fail to recognize the value of a single hour. Good things come in small packages.

2. Retreat can take place while coursing down the highway at 70 mph. It can take place sitting on a park bench, in public or in private, on the beach, in a coffee shop, in the woods, on a roof, in a boat, in your favorite chair at home.

3. You can retreat with a friend or a small group. The solitary nature of retreat prevents many people from engaging, but it's an unnecessary roadblock. Jesus' retreat time often included others (Matthew 17:1, Luke 22:39-41). Enjoy the camaraderie of traveling together and shared meals, but go your separate ways for times of rest, reflection, prayer, exploration. Enjoy your time of fellowship with God. Enjoy your time of fellowship with your friend or spouse.

4. Retreat will include things that allow you to tap into the deep resources of God. But recognize the value of "R & R" (rest and relaxation). Take time to unwind. For some, that may require many hours. Most of us are wound

tighter than a top. Feast. Nap. Hike. If you're at a retreat center, take time to boat, read, fish, stargaze or shoot some hoops. Allow it to be a day of delight.

5. Retreat demands an open heart. Don't come with great expectations. You might leave disappointed. Come with a surrendered heart, intent on the desire, *"Find rest, O, my soul in God alone."* (Psalm 62:5) Your cup will overflow.

Food For Thought:

1. When planning a personal retreat, ask a friend to join you. As the day draws near and the stress of life mounts, it is easy to renege, but much harder if you've invited a friend. Enjoy your time together, but prioritize portions of your time to be alone with God.

2. If you're looking for a retreat center, check out *Christian Camp and Conference Association.* Many camps and retreat centers don't have a formal personal retreat ministry, but most will open their doors and put out the welcome mat. For retreat centers near you, check out www.ccca.org

3. Allow retreat to become an intentional rhythm, an offensive, strategic priority in your life. Commit to a time of retreat once a year, once a season, or once a month. Tie your retreat experience to a yearly event: your birthday, your favorite month of the year, Labor Day, New Year's Day.

Red pen.
Pick a date and a manageable time-frame.
Consider a favorite place.
Childcare? Tag team or divide and conquer!

Finally – listen well to the One who calls to your heart.
> *"Come with Me by yourselves to a quiet place and get some rest."*
> Mark 6:31 NIV

Make it Your Own

As you consider going on retreat, what ideas surprise you?

Are you willing to commit? Can you pick a day? Invite a friend?

Don't delay.

Plan B

I am on retreat today. It is a *defensive* retreat based on a breaking heart, diminishing returns and the beginning of an intense season of ministry for my family. (It was May when I wrote this. We run a Christian summer camp.) My retreat was going to take place at a city park beside a small lake with a trip to a favorite coffee shop.

Instead, it is taking place in the hospital room of my 19-year old son, Josh, who was admitted last night. It's Josh's 69th night in the hospital over the last 9 ½ months. We are in a long-haul, very hard season.

In my life – again and again – the power, peace and Presence of God is most fully accessed in a quiet hour off the beaten path – no matter where I am and what's going on.

> *I will give you treasures of darkness, riches stored in secret places, so that you may know that I am the Lord, the God of Israel, who calls you by name.*
> Isaiah 45:3 NIV

Plan A.
Plan B.
One way or the other, I pray you make time for retreat in the next few weeks. Begin with a quiet hour or two.

You will find yourself on holy ground.

The power, peace and presence of God is most fully accessed in a quiet hour off the beaten path - no matter where I am and what's going on.

Make it Your Own

What kind of plan might you make for *offensive* retreat rhythms in your life?

> Once a year.
> Once a season.
> Once a month for a quiet few hours.
> What do you hear God inviting you to embrace?
> Make it a matter of prayer.

Are you in need of a *defensive* retreat? Are the red flags of overload flapping in the wind? Carve out two quiet hours <u>this</u> week. Commit to it as if your life depends on it. It probably does.

The Heavens Declare

Do you love a little person in your life – or a bunch of little people ages 0-18? (They don't even have to live under your roof.) This post is for you.

Think

Why do we spend most of our prayer time *talking* to God? Talking *to* God is predictable. I know the routine. I sit in the driver's seat. I know what to expect. But it falls short. Something is missing.

Why does monologue prayer come so easily to us? Because that's what we were taught. It's relatively easy to teach kids to *talk* to God, except for a handful of thoughtful kids who announce, "How am I supposed to talk to Someone I can't see?"

Dialogue, however, is a whole 'nother ball game. While monologue is predictable, teaching kids to dialogue with God is potentially unwieldy. Be still before God? Listen? That's not easy. It hints of mystery and could get messy.

"How am I supposed to talk to someone I can't see?"

"How in the world do I teach a child to be still, to *know* God, to listen?"
"What if I show kids how to be still, to listen to God and He doesn't say anything?"
"What if they hear something I don't think God said? What then?"
Those are questions we have to ask and wrestle through, but there's one that undergirds them all.

Have *you* ever been taught how to be still in the presence of God? Have you ever taught your kids to be still in the presence of God? It's easier than you might think. Make a date to *retreat* outside on a star-studded night.

Prepare

Preparing the next generation to *retreat*, to listen to God requires some forethought:

1. Ground your kids in God's Word. Every day share with them what He is saying to you through His Word. Ask them what He's saying to them.

2. Learn to "be still and know" yourself. Become familiar and comfortable with stillness. *Guard your steps when you go to the house of God. Go near to listen rather than to offer the sacrifice of fools, who do not know that they do wrong.* Ecclesiastes 5:1 NIV The work of stillness – of listening to God – is tied to the work of the Holy Spirit. Spend some time in John 14-16. A good starting place is John 14:15-20.

3. The word for *spirit* in the Bible is linked to breath and wind. Do a word study and share your insights with your children. Pay attention to the wind. It has much to teach us.

Launch

1. Sometime this month, carve out some outside *retreat* time with your favorite little person – or big person. Immerse yourself in the sanctuary of God – together. There is no better place for stillness or attentiveness to the Presence of God. Lie in the grass. Watch the clouds. Count the stars. Bask before a sunset. Share your heart. Tell them about your own (old or new) journey of learning how to retreat, how to be still before God. You don't have to have all the answers. Just share your heart. Read Psalm 19:1-4. Then read Psalm 95:1-7. Close in prayer. "Dear Jesus, help us be still and know You are God." Then be still.

2. Keep in mind – we are not responsible for what God does or doesn't do in stillness in the hearts of our children.

We must release the reins. He is God. We can trust His handiwork.

Make it Your Own

Are you able or willing to set a time for an outside retreat? With a child (or alone) consider an hour outside with God ... day or night. No Bible. No material. Just you and God, stillness and the grandeur of His creation.

Has the Lord placed children in your life to love? Train? Disciple? Yours? Others? We have a job to do. Psalm 71:18 NIV speaks to us today. *"Even when I'm old and gray, do not forsake me, O God, till I declare Your power to the next generation, Your might to all who are to come."*
That's a tall order. We've got a job to do. Let's begin with a life-lesson on retreat and stillness.

What makes this challenge attractive? Difficult?

Week 5 - Connections

1. Have you ever been on retreat? Was it offensive in nature? Defensive? Forced? Tell us about the gifts it offered you.

2. What three practical ideas will impact your commitment or ability to go on retreat?

Parting Word

Read Psalm 63:1-5. Take note of the introduction. Was David on retreat?

  Allow a minute of silent prayer and reflection.

Read Psalm 63:1-5 again.

Share your thoughts.

Close in a time of prayer.

6 Running the Race
Vantage Point | Trek 6

Convicted!

255 people enter this world every minute.*107 people die every minute. And 73 people die without knowing Jesus Christ.
By the time you finish reading this devotional thought, 150 people will have died without knowing Christ.

This statistic makes me swallow hard. It drives me to a quiet, reflective place. We have work to do. The ministry of *Run Hard. Rest Well.* exists so we are able to run our race in strength, with a purpose and vibrancy not our own. Rest is delightful in every way, but rest was crafted for a purpose. A divine purpose.

We *are* running a race, but too often it feels like a treadmill. The *rat race* robs us. The price tag is hefty. To run our race and run it well, we need to revisit the truth behind four key words: Conviction. Commission. Commitments. Calling.

Conviction

Conviction is an invitation and a driving force to prioritize our life in a way that is directed and empowered by the Holy Spirit. Left to ourselves, comfort, convenience and self-absorption nudge their way into our thinking, our doing, our values and our calendars. None of us are immune.

> **Rest is delightful in every way, but rest was crafted for a purpose. A divine purpose.**

Do I live under the deep conviction that God is the Potter and that I am a vessel made *on* purpose *for* a purpose?

> *"For I know the plans I have for you,"*
> *declares the Lord ..."*
> Jeremiah 29:11a NIV
> *"May the favor of the Lord our God rest upon us; establish the work of our hands for us — yes, establish the work of our hands."*
> Psalm 90:17 NIV
> *"The Lord **will** (my emphasis) fulfill His purpose for me; your love, O Lord, endures forever — do not abandon the works of Your hand."* Psalm 138:8 NIV

Take home

1. The motivation behind God's purpose is love.
2. His purposes for us are long-term endeavors. It takes determination on both ends. God is good to go. Are we? Are we determined to live under the conviction that God has a plan for our lives above and beyond convenience and comfort?

> *These figures were gleaned from Wholesome Words website based on 2014 statistics. To view this information on-line, visit wholecomewords.org/missions/greatc. html. Tuck these truths into your heart and keep them before you. We run the race, not for numbers, but for real-life people with names, faces, and a place in God's heart.

Make it Your Own

Do comfort, convenience and self-absorption dominate the landscape of your life?

Some have said that the number one idol of American Christians is the happiness and success of our children. What do you think?

How much time and energy goes into praying for and spending time with, each week, those who do not know the love of Christ?

Commissioned

You have been commissioned to participate in the Great Commission. So have I. It's **the** commission … *"Go and make disciples of all nations"* Matthew 28:19 NIV. We are all aware of it, but few take it seriously.

Our fruit is meager.
Our guilt is real, then quickly diverted by the demands and distractions of this world.

My daughter, Anna, at the age of six nailed it on the head. "Mommy, is the most important thing about being a Christian telling other people about Jesus?"

"Yes!" I announced. My internal monologue kicked in. "Anna gets it! I'm doing a good job."

My self-affirmation was short lived.
"Then, why don't you do it very often?"

She called a spade a spade.
Anna had heard me "preach to the choir" a hundred times in her short life. But she was right; she had never once heard me share my faith with someone who did not know Jesus.

Go

It was one of Jesus' last words and it's a word – a commission – that needs to be taken to heart.
It's not about distance, however. *Going* overseas is not better than *going* across the street.

> It's not about distance, however. Going overseas is not better than going across the street.

"Go" is about determination and it takes intentionality.

It's all about love. But love takes time and most of us live in the red. We have "no time."

Programmed church activities are a great use of gifts and are a part of our calling, but left unchecked they require enormous amounts of our "free time" – leaving little margin to commit to the time consuming work of getting to know and loving another human being or a family of human begins.

Programs don't bring people to Christ. People bring people to Christ. Programs are predictable. (Be there from 6-8 pm.) People are messy and unpredictable.

Programs don't bring people to Christ. People bring people to Christ.

Nine times out of ten, being a part of the Great Commission is about developing intentional friendships. It's about taking the time to get to know someone. It's about sharing life over the long haul, on the soccer field, at work, in your neighbor's garage. It's about earning the right *and* the opportunity to share your heart and ask life-changing questions. It happens quite naturally when love is established and the time is right and ripe.

Operation Go
It's a matter of love, not obligation.
It takes time. It takes margin. Embracing the rhythm *Run hard. Rest well* is a great place to start.

Make it Your Own

Who's on your radar? A cousin? A co-worker? A neighbor? Make love – with no strings attached – your aim. Set your sights long. Stay on your knees.

Want a game plan?

1. Who is God laying on your heart? Commit them to prayer. If appropriate, invite your kids to pray as well. Include them in on the *commissioning*.
2. Choose the use of your time prayerfully and intentionally. Don't overextend.
3. Rest well.
4. Then let love lead the way. Pick up the phone. Send a text. Walk across the street. Get together. Seek to serve, laugh, enjoy. Regularly.

The best time to start? Today.

Who has God laid on your heart?

Commitments and Calling

Each season of our life is made up of a unique blend of *commitments* and *calling*.

Commitments

Commitments are the non-negotiable obligations in our life. Some bring great joy, like caring for a long-awaited newborn. Some are expected: putting bread on the table, gas in the car and a roof over head. Some are hard: paying off debt incurred by a reckless ex-spouse, providing life-time care for a special-needs child, attending to the 24/7 care of a dying loved one.

These commitments fuel our transformation. God wastes nothing. Some of His best work happens in the hottest fires.

Three things to keep in mind:
1. Soften your heart to the work transformation, even if you go into it kicking and screaming.
2. Trust God.
3. Tell of His goodness. Be ready to give an account of your hope. It can be awfully hard on the days when the trio *rugged, brutal* and *grueling* are pulling you under. Truly, God does some of his best work in times of immense heat and pressure.

Last year, on day six of what turned into a 19-day hospital stay with my 15-year-old son, Joe, I began to question God. "Do you know all the ministry opportunities I'm missing at home?"

"Do you know how many you're missing right *here*?"

I wasn't fully convinced. Being three hours from home, my heart was breaking for my other four children who were depleted, weary and overwhelmed.

"Lord, Joe can't take the pain. I can't take watching him in anguish. My kids at home are on their last leg."

"I'm working on *them*, too. They're learning how to trust. They'll have something to tell. *Trust and tell.* Give it a try."

God was right.

The harder the trust factor, the greater the story. God lands on center stage. He promises stories for us to share of His presence and provision. Our commitment to our commitments will bring glory to God.

Calling

Our calling (which can change from season to season) makes use of our negotiable "free" time. It may be what we get paid to do. It may be what we "do" on a volunteer basis. It may be a dream in the making. It's where our gifts, energy and passion collide with a need. Teaching ESL. Coaching. Playing drums. Sending notes. Making things work.

What energizes you? Kayaking? Reading? Carpentry? Knitting? Travel? Organizing? Cars?

The world tells us to "go for it" with gusto, but the ensuing pursuit is sometimes self-centered. In the end, my passion consumes hours, but it's all about me, myself, and I.

How can the "thing" that energizes me build bridges to new friends? Meet a need? Cast a vision? Serve those who are marginalized, neglected, forgotten?

God is ready to tell us.
But we need to ask.

Pay attention. Listen well. This is where rest comes in. Quiet places attune our hearts to whispers and marching orders.

Rest replenishes us for the race we run.
Quiet directs our steps.

Make it Your Own

What commitments fill your days? How do they delight you? Deplete you? How are you learning to "trust and tell?"

Calling. Can you name your calling for this season of your life?

Onward

Now the journey really begins.

Rest is a matter of obedience, stewardship and delight.

My journey into rhythms of rest and restoration began in 1990. It continues. It's a journey that includes growth, setbacks, maturity and an ever-expanding desire to equip others to explore this road less traveled.

It is my prayer and the prayer of many that this study blesses you, encourages you and alters the course of your life and the lives of those you influence.

I have two things to ask of you.

One. Continue on. Don't give up and don't give in to the pressure of overload and exhaustion. Satan will try to discourage you. He knows, all too well, that rest taps into the storehouses of God. Don't let a feeling of defeat cripple you. Enjoy and celebrate every hour of rest for the gift that it is. Commit to the journey of rhythm, rest and restoration found in Sleep, Sabbath, Stillness and Solitude. It will be a life-long endeavor of joy and delight.

Two. Recognize that you are a person of influence. Share stories. Invite others to join this journey. Too many people are running on empty. Plant seeds. Point the

way. Encourage. Cheer each
other on.

I believe the ministry of *Run hard. Rest well*
is a movement of God. It has been birthed
in the furnace of adversity, drenched in
tears and heartbreak. In the end, I would
have it no other way. My desperation
became the arena of His deliverance. I
believe the message of rest, released in the
lives of God's people is the critical, missing
ingredient for revival in our hearts, our
families, our neighborhoods, our world.

Pass it on – out loud. The church-at-large
has much to learn about the power and
purpose of rest. It begins with dialogue,
discussion, exploration, honest assessment.
The hunger is there. We need to direct
people to the feast.

Pass it on in the vibrant life of a life well-
lived.

Run hard. Break a sweat every day.

Rest well. In fullness. In freedom. On fire
for the Living God.

Make it Your Own

Did you need the message of *Run hard. Rest well* at this point in your life? Did it come at a good time?

What will change? What do you fear may stay the same?

Take a look at the "groups" of people listed on pages 7-9. Which of these groups do you see yourself playing a role in introducing them to the motto and message *Run hard. Rest well* formally or informally? Why are you drawn to that group? What's step #1?

Week 6 - Connections

1. Many of us need a wake-up call in regards to *the* purpose of our lives. It's too easy to adopt the priorities of those around us (inside and outside the church), priorities that do not keep the "main thing" the main thing. Here are a couple of hard questions.

2. How does "the church" keep us from being salt and light? What are you going to do about it?

3. What are your chief commitments right now?

4. What is your calling?
> Our *calling* uses our gifts, spotlights our priorities and provides an avenue to steward our time well. There are seasons of life where there may be little time to pursue our calling. *Wait* is one the hardest, holiest words there is. Is *wait* a part of your life right now?

5. When embracing our calling (paid, volunteer or in-waiting), burnout will nip at our heels. Satan cheers when we forfeit the race. Sustainability matters. Rest is the key. Rhythm provides a routine oasis along the way.
> Would you agree?

6. Can you name the 4 *Rhythms of Rest*?

7. Which one has impacted you the most over the last few weeks?

You are a person of influence. You have an opportunity to mentor and model a better way. Who will be most "challenged to change" by your example, encouragement and informal or formal teaching? Are you ready to invite others to rediscover the Rest and Race we are meant to enjoy?

Parting Word

Read Jeremiah 6:16.

Allow a minute of silent prayer and reflection.

Read Jeremiah 6:16 again.

Share your thoughts.

Close in a time of prayer.

Closing Thought

Dear friends,

The journey has begun.

We pray it continues.

Learning to embrace restorative rhythms of rest is a matter of life and death. When biblical rest is not woven into the fabric of our lives, death by overload or distraction will dictate the demise of the things we hold dear – the depth and breadth of our dreams, the quality of our relationships, the intimacy we enjoy with the Father, and/or the vibrancy of our physical and emotional health.

By and large, the beliefs and behaviors of overload have been engrained in us for decades. It will take some energy and effort to see new life take root and grow. Three commitments strengthen our resolve.

1. Make a plan to build accountability into your life. Chose a traveling companion (possibly from this group) who has an authentic, compassionate heart. Once or twice a month, check in with each other. Consider using the Inventory from page 14 as a starting point. Follow the Spirit's lead. Take time to pray.

2. Target someone to teach. Ask the Lord who that might be. Share your story, your journey and what you've been learning along the way. Maybe working through this study guide is a good place to begin.

3. Consider joining the RHRW community and conversation. It takes place over a short, encouraging, weekly blog post via email or Facebook.

My prayers and the prayers of the entire RHRW team are with you. Feel free to connect. We'd love to hear from you. Additional books and resources are also available. Onward, dear friend. Onward and upward! brenda@runhardrestwell.com

Jesus leads the way.

Brenda

References

Bounds, E.M. (2009). *The works of E.M. Bound.* Zeeland, MI:
    Reformed Church Publications.

Center for Disease Control (2015). The benefits of physical
    activity. Retrieved from http://www.cdc.gov/
    physicalactivity/everyone/health/index.html

Figueiro, M.G., Wood B., Plitnick B., Rea M.S. (2011). The impact
    of light from computer monitors on melatonin levels in
    college students. *Neuro Endocrinology Letters*, 32(2),
    158-63. Retrieved from http://www.ncbi.nlm.nih.gov/
    pubmed/21552190

Leproult R., Copinschi G., Buxton O., & Van Cauter E. (1997).
    Sleep loss results in an elevation of cortisol levels the next
    evening. *Sleep*, 20(10), 865-870. Retrieved from http://
    www.ncbi.nlm.nih.gov/pubmed/9415946

Narcotics Anonymous, The Basic Text (1992). Van Nuys, CA,
    U.S.A : World Service Office.

National Sleep Foundation (2011). Annual sleep in America poll
    exploring connections with communications technology
    use and sleep. Retrieved from https://sleepfoundation.org/
    media-center/press-release/annual-sleep-america-poll-
    exploring-connections-communications-technology-use-

Niebuhr, R. (n.d). *The serenity prayer*. Retrieved from https://
en.wikipedia.org/wiki/Serenity_Prayer

Reynolds, G. (2012). How exercise could lead to a better brain.
The New York Times Magazine. Retrieved from http://www.
nytimes.com/2012/04/22/magazine/how-exercise-could-
lead-to-a-better-brain.html?_r=1

Stevens, B. (1977). ""The truth shall make you free, but first it
shall make you miserable." Retrieved from http://www.
barrypopik.com/index.php/new_york_city/entry/the_truth_
will_set_you_free_but_first_it_will_make_you_miserable

Sumioka, H., Nakae, A., Kanai, R., & Ishiguro, H. (2013).
Huggable communication medium decreases cortisol
levels. *Scientific Reports*, 3. doi: doi:10.1038/srep03034.
Retrieved from http://www.nature.com/articles/srep03034

Voskamp, A. (2011). *One thousand gifts: A dare to live fully right
where you are*. Grand Rapids, MI: Zondervan.

Weinhouse, B. (2015, March). America's sleep crisis is making
us sick, fat, and stupid. But there's hope. *Readers Digest*.
Retrieved from http://www.rd.com/health/conditions/
america-sleep-crisis/

Notes

Scripture

Journaling

Journaling